20 FUN FACTS ABOUT
DRAGONFLIES

By Maria Nelson

Please visit our website, www.garethstevens.com. For a free color catalog of all our high-quality books, call toll free 1-800-542-2595 or fax 1-877-542-2596.

Library of Congress Cataloging-in-Publication Data

Nelson, Maria.
 20 fun facts about dragonflies / Maria Nelson.
     p. cm. — (Fun fact file: bugs!)
 Includes index.
 ISBN 978-1-4339-8236-1 (pbk.)
 ISBN 978-1-4339-8237-8 (6-pack)
 ISBN 978-1-4339-8235-4 (library binding)
 1. Dragonflies—Juvenile literature. I. Title. II. Title: Twenty fun facts about dragonflies.
 QL520.N44 2013
 595.7'33—dc23
                                        2012021207

First Edition

Published in 2013 by
Gareth Stevens Publishing
111 East 14th Street, Suite 349
New York, NY 10003

Copyright © 2013 Gareth Stevens Publishing

Designer: Benjamin Gardner
Editor: Greg Roza

Photo credits: Cover, p. 1 Michael Sewell Visual Pursuit/Peter Arnold/Getty Images; p. 5 Dudarev Mikhail/Shutterstock.com; p. 6 Tomas Sereda/Shutterstock.com; pp. 7, 27 Claffra/Shutterstock.com; p. 8 Photography by Shin T/Flickr/Getty Images; p. 9 Nikitin Mikhail/Shutterstock.com; p. 10 Melinda Fawver/Shutterstock.com; p. 11 Federico Stevanin/ Shutterstock.com; p. 12 Brad Thompson/Shutterstock.com; p. 13 Chantal De Bruijne/ Shutterstock.com; p. 14 Jessica Billings/Shutterstock.com; p. 15 Rene Krekels/Foto Natura/ Minden Pictures/Getty Images; p. 16 Tom Branch/Photo Researchers/Getty Images; p. 17 Gucio_55/Shutterstock.com; p. 18 Vaklav/Shutterstock.com; p. 19 night_cat/ Shutterstock.com; p. 20 Worldswildlifewonders/Shutterstock.com; p. 21 Biker11/Shutterstock. com; p. 22 A. S. Floro/Shutterstock.com; p. 23 Lane V. Erickson/Shutterstock.com; p. 24 (damselfly)Wansfordphoto/Shutterstock.com; p. 24 (dragonfly) Alslutsky/ Shutterstock.com; p. 26 NitroCephal/Shutterstock.com; p. 29 Stefady/Flcikr/Getty Images.

Printed in the United States of America

CPSIA compliance information: Batch #CW13GS: For further information contact Gareth Stevens, New York, New York at 1-800-542-2595.

Contents

Words in the glossary appear in **bold** type the first time they are used in the text.

Life on the Wing

With its two pairs of pretty wings, a dragonfly looks graceful as it flies around its pond or lake home. Did you know the dragonfly is also a swift and deadly **predator**? From its six legs to the many lenses of its eyes, some of the coolest dragonfly features help it catch **prey**.

There are about 2,500 species, or kinds, of dragonflies. Whether you're in your backyard or on vacation in Africa or India, you might see these amazing insects!

A dragonfly rests on a plant near a pond.

Let Your Colors Show

FACT 1

Dragonflies can be as colorful as butterflies.

From yellows and reds to browns and blues, dragonflies can show some wild colors. They might look shiny or even be spotted! While some species of dragonfly are more colorful than others, each dragonfly has its own special look.

This red dragonfly is called a vagrant darter.

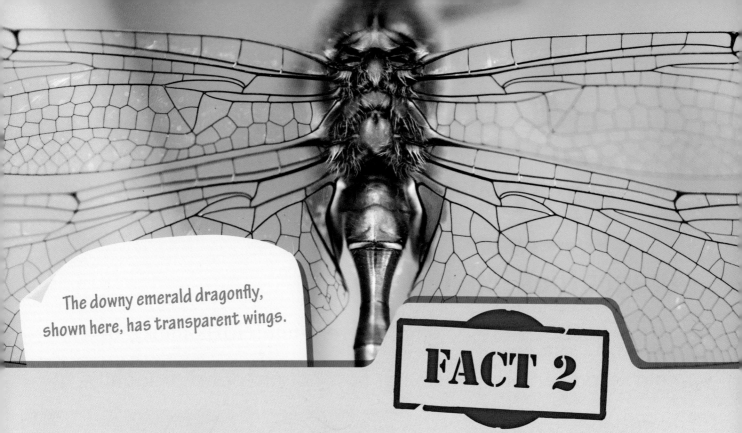

The downy emerald dragonfly, shown here, has transparent wings.

FACT 2

Dragonfly wings may look weak, but they're actually rather tough.

Some of a dragonfly's coloring may come from its beautiful wings. **Transparent** as well as colorful, their wings are strong—even if they don't look it. Dragonflies commonly have a **wingspan** between about 0.8 inch (2 cm) and almost 8 inches (20 cm).

Sun Lovers

FACT 3

Dragonflies like it hot!

Dragonflies are ectothermic (ehk-tuh-THUHR-mihk), or cold-blooded. This means that how hot or cold a dragonfly is depends on its surroundings. You'll see the most dragonflies on warm, sunny days—that's what they like best!

A sunny summer day is your best chance to see a dragonfly.

Dragonflies use the sun to get moving.

Dragonfly wings work best when they're warm. In the morning, you might see a dragonfly perched on a leaf, soaking up some sun, or beating its wings very quickly to warm up. They like the sun so much they might not even come out on cool or cloudy days!

Super Fliers

FACT 5

A dragonfly could keep up with a moving car on a city street.

Dragonflies are fast. They can reach speeds of about 35 miles (56 km) per hour. The southern giant darner dragonfly is known as the fastest flying insect. Dragonflies are such good fliers that scientists have built robots modeled to fly like them!

Have you ever seen a dragonfly hover in the air? It can be an awesome sight.

FACT 6

A dragonfly uses its wings to fly around—or stay put.

Dragonflies have two sets of wings. They can move these together or separately. This movement allows dragonflies to fly up, down, or backward, and make quick turns. They can also **hover** like a helicopter!

FACT 7

Dragonflies can hide while flying.

Dragonflies use **agile** flying to avoid predators. Some dragonflies can copy the tiny motions of a watchful predator so quickly and exactly that the predator can't even see them move! This hides them from animals looking for movement that could mean a snack.

Dragonflies catch their prey while flying.

In ponds without big fish, dragonflies may be the top predator. Dragonflies are carnivores, or meat eaters. However, the meat they eat isn't chicken or a hamburger! Dragonflies use their feet to catch mosquitoes, gnats, and even dragonflies smaller than themselves.

This dragonfly has caught a yellow ladybug for lunch.

FACT 9

The globe skimmer dragonfly travels 11,000 miles (17,700 km) round-trip!

Many kinds of dragonflies **migrate**. These species are avoiding cold weather or flying to places that are good for **mating**. In 2010, a scientist studied the migration of the globe skimmer. These dragonflies fly from India, across the Indian Ocean, to east Africa.

FACT 10

Dragonflies start their life in freshwater.

Dragonflies hatch from eggs laid in or near freshwater. After adult dragonflies mate, females lay hundreds of round eggs. Depending on the species, these eggs are about 0.02 to 0.04 inch (0.5 to 1 mm) across.

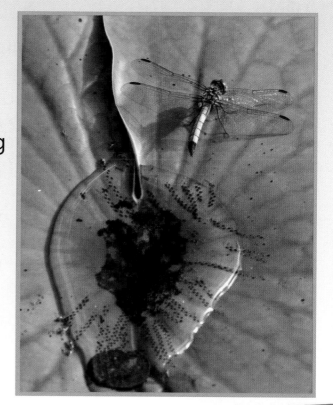

This dragonfly is laying eggs on a lily pad.

FACT 11

Dragonfly nymphs use gills to move and breathe.

Dragonfly **larvae** are called nymphs. These young dragonflies have six skinny legs, two big eyes, and a small body. Nymphs breathe in water using gills, like a fish does. By pushing water out through these gills, nymphs can jet through the water!

This dragonfly nymph is resting on a plant underwater.

A dragonfly without wings is still a predator.

Dragonflies may remain nymphs for several months or more than a year. Nymphs use pinching mouthparts to catch prey, such as other insects and even tiny fish. Nymphs eat lots of prey so they can grow—and eventually get their wings.

FACT 13

Dragonfly nymphs may shed their skin up to 20 times.

As nymphs grow, they molt, or shed their skin. It's during its many molts that a dragonfly's wings first appear. When it's big enough, the nymph crawls out of the water and molts one last time.

This nymph is ready to become an adult.

The Life Cycle of the Dragonfly

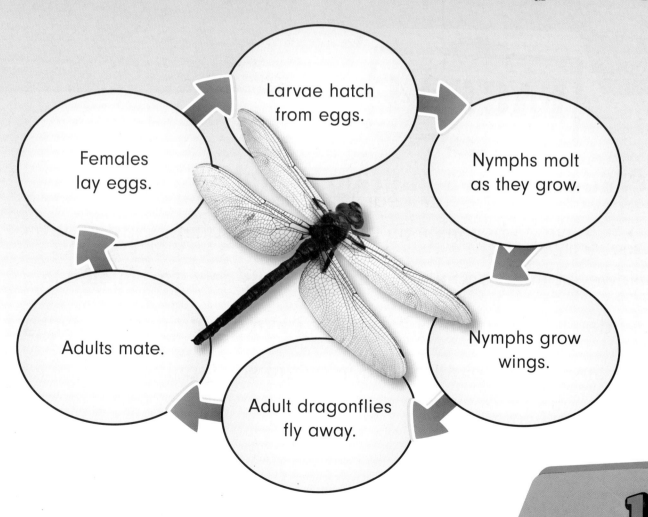

Larvae hatch from eggs.

Nymphs molt as they grow.

Females lay eggs.

Nymphs grow wings.

Adults mate.

Adult dragonflies fly away.

A gecko got to this dragonfly before its exoskeleton could harden.

FACT 14

Predators love molting nymphs.

A nymph becomes an adult dragonfly after its last molt. However, the dragonfly has to wait for its new **exoskeleton** to harden before it can fly. Predators eat many dragonflies during this time. Ducks, big fish, and frogs are some animals that enjoy a dragonfly meal!

FACT 15

Dragonflies can see almost all the way around their heads.

Dragonflies have sharp eyesight to help them catch prey. Much of their head is taken up with two large eyes. Each eye is made up of almost 30,000 lenses. About 80 percent of a dragonfly's brain is used for sight!

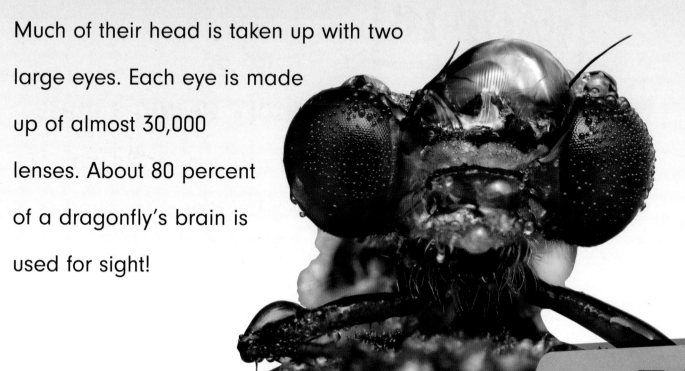

FACT 16

Male dragonflies need territory to win a mate.

Female dragonflies want to mate with a male that has territory right on a pond or lake. This allows her many good places to lay eggs. Male dragonflies will fight off other males to guard this territory and their mate.

Want to know if an area is healthy? Look for dragonflies!

Different species of dragonflies like different bodies of water. However, dragonflies only live and mate near freshwater that's clean and in areas that don't have a lot of pollution. Pollution affects some species more than others, but seeing dragonflies is commonly a good sign!

A dragonfly skims along the surface of a pond.

What's in a Name?

Dragonflies have look-alikes.

Are you sure you're looking at a dragonfly—and not a

damselfly? Dragonflies are part of the scientific group Odonata.

These insects have
large eyes, two pairs
of transparent wings,
and a long, thin
body. Damselflies are
odonates, too!

damselfly

dragonfly

Damselflies rest with their wings together, while dragonflies rest with their wings apart.

Comparing Dragonfiles and Damselflies

dragonflies

rests with wings apart

eggs are round

nymph's gills inside the body

both

two large eyes

two pairs of transparent wings

first stage of life in water

hatches from egg

long, thin body

damselflies

rests with wings together

eggs are tube shaped

nymph's gills at the end of the body

This is a dragonfly fossil trapped in amber. Amber is hardened tree sap.

FACT 19

The first insects linked to dragonflies lived on Earth before the dinosaurs.

Scientists have found remains, or fossils, of a group of insects called Protodonata that are more than 325 million years old. These bugs looked a lot like modern dragonflies, but had a wingspan of up to 30 inches (75 cm)!

Dragonflies have some colorful nicknames. They're sometimes called the devil's darning needle.

An old story about dragonflies says that children who tell lies would have their lips sewn shut by the insect! This explains a few of the names dragonflies are known as, such as darner, which means one who mends with needle and thread, or devil's darning needle.

Dragonflies Around the World

From their beautiful colors to their amazing flying skills, dragonflies are cool bugs! Since they're found all over the world—except in Antarctica—people of many countries have stories and ideas about them.

In Japan, dragonflies are more than just something pretty to look at in the garden. They're a sign of power and victory. The Chinese see dragonflies as good luck charms! Native American tribes link dragonflies with speed and happiness. Wherever they're found, dragonflies will brighten anyone's day!

This is a close up of a dragonfly called a red-veined darter.

29

Glossary

agile: able to move quickly and easily

exoskeleton: the hard outer covering of an animal's body

hover: to float in the air without moving around much

larvae: bugs in an early life stage that have a wormlike form

mate: to come together to make babies. Also, one of two animals that come together to make babies.

migrate: to move from one area to another for feeding or having babies

predator: an animal that hunts other animals for food

prey: an animal that is hunted by other animals for food

transparent: able to be seen through

wingspan: the length between the tips of a pair of wings that are stretched out

For More Information

Books

Creese, Sarah. *Bugs.* Nashville, TN: Make Believe Ideas, 2010.

Hudak, Heather C. *Dragonflies.* New York, NY: Weigl Publishers, 2009.

Rissman, Rebecca. *Dragonflies.* Chicago, IL: Raintree Publishing, 2013.

Websites

Critter Catalog: Dragonflies
www.biokids.umich.edu/critters/Anisoptera/pictures/
This website has many pictures of different kinds of dragonflies and lots of amazing facts.

Insect: Dragonfly
kids.sandiegozoo.org/animals/insects/dragonfly
See cool pictures of dragonflies and learn more about these and other insects.

Index